Timeless Friendships

Rachana Raut

BookLeaf Publishing

Presentation by *BookLeaf Publishing*

Web: www.bookleafpub.com

E-mail: info@bookleafpub.com

ISBN: 9789357741828

First edition 2023

*To my friends, who chose to love every bit
of me.*

ACKNOWLEDGEMENT

There are lot of people I met and whom I am grateful for inspiring the noble idea of this book. But to mention a few, my first thanks to those friends who chose to stay and fight for our friendship even with years that came by. Thanks to my college friends Shreyanka, Sanjyot, Sakshi and others who let me rely on them when I needed them. To my school friend Sheetal, who showed me the innocence of a friendship formed in early age can be maintained even in your adult years. Finally, a thank you to my parents for believing that I can make things happen in my life and inculcating my interests in books and reading.

PREFACE

One of the first relationships that we form from early years beside with our parents and siblings are friendships. This book pays homage to those friends who continues to keep the kind, innocent value of the word friendship and decide to keep nurturing it ahead! For those who are not related to us by blood but decide to do it by choice.

Listen, I have to tell you…

Swimming in a mindless dream, suddenly a song
starts playing
I wonder if I have heard it and find my phone
blaring,
I wake up immediately to see 2.45am on the
clock that is ticking
Who would call me so late I marvel, and see
your name flash on my screen with eyes blurring
I pick up the call immediately, half curious, half
scared
What is this news that couldn't wait
"Listen, I have to tell you something…" I hear
the breathy voice
"What happened!" I ask aloud
"I feel lonely today, and you are what I miss
talking with the most" in small voice I hear
I sit straight on my bed and hear myself say, "Do
you want to talk about it my dear?"
"Yes, it's been a while since I met my friends"
you express with sadness
All at once we both are in our college corridors
painting reminiscent canvases
Laughing, talking and watching in muted silence
of our memories of the days that are gone

"Do you remember…?" we ask each other for an
hour
"Sorry, I woke you up so late" you whisper
I remark, "What are friends, that aren't for
midnight calls and be a listener"
With bittersweet feeling in our heart, we keep
the phone down
The time tells me it's 4am, time for dawn
With a smile, I pull my blanket over
And experience myself slipping in those echoes
of an old classroom in the month of October

Long time, No see?

Flipping through the photo album, I see at our
young beaming faces
Stuck in that moment of our tender ages
I close the album and realize with amazement
"Where are you now?" with each passing
moment
The last time we met was some years back,
You looked happy but I wasn't sure with time's
lost track
I wonder if you remember me, remember us
Those tiffin breaks, standing outside the class or
waiting for our bus
Do you think about those games we played
About the promises we made
Of never letting our bond break
And covering for each other's mistake
Forgotten in the sands of time
These reminders of us seem sublime
Will we ever see each other in the lost crowd
Cross each other and say "Long time, no see?!"
aloud
For now, I don't know if that will ever happen
The meeting of two old friends with same
beaming faces again

The first meeting

I had my headphones on, listening to a random
song,
Lost in my thoughts, escaping the reality for too
long
As I closed my eyes on the drop of the beat,
In you came, and flopped down on the close by
seat,
Next thing I knew a hand extended towards me,
You just went on to introduce yourself so
brightly
Shocked and magnetized by your careless air,
I said "Hi" and introduced myself with
conviction and dare,
And then you said, there are more of you and me
out in the world
The vibe and the wavelength between two of us
swirled
Who knew in that first meeting I would reach a
day
Where you would be my safe haven to share my
gloom and gay

Enemies to Lovers? Enemies to Best Friend!

In the world of enemies to lovers,
We became enemies to best friend
From throwing each other out of the school
classroom,
To throwing arms around each other,
From innocently challenging each other,
To courageously support each other to go for
things in life
From having those crying sessions on the
terraces,
To assuring that life will get around
With each passing year,
We learned, we grew, but most importantly
We became each other's sanctuary
And nobody can change my mind,
This will always be the best trope in the real
world

House of Sins

For every house of sin, a friend brought a virtue
in my life,
Each stuck with me like a deep embedded knife
For Wrath,
One showed me kindness,
For Sloth,
One gave me courage
For Envy,
One taught me companionship
For Lust,
One embraced me with innocence
For Pride,
One grounded me to my roots
For Gluttony,
One taught me moderation and balance
For Greed,
One gave me immense love
But unbeknownst of all the sins
Each one freed me from the chains
For seven sins, there was a seven colored
rainbow of hope
Each of you brought it with you and scattered
around me like a kaleidoscope

A friend in my colleague

In the setup of office, we usually give
appreciations
But what about those colleagues,
Who are more than those awards and
recognitions
Colleagues, who are not only available for a
weekday support call,
But when available for random catchup calls, or
to join our next vacations
And unknowingly the corporate life doesn't
seem that daunting
We meet in workplaces and soon find ourselves
standing at the same pickup stations

We are workplace associates,
But more than that we end up calling each other
as workplace-buddies
All that mirth and laughter shared
Gives those stressful hours of 9 to 5 a partner
who cares
And all in all, in the world of soulmates,
Somewhere you find yourself sitting beside a
workmate

Vacation

To every plan that was made,
To every plan that got cancelled,
To every promise of the next time,
And every chat group with new trip name
We all promised for a time that will come
When we all will go out together and make it
happen
But those were the days when we were together
every moment
In classrooms and cafeterias
Sipping drinks and laughing as no time has
passed

Years later, now when we yearn for those plans
to form
With every message that comes from those lost
friends about a meetup
And this time when we all say yes,
We know how much these outings mean
The value of time spent is immeasurable
But somethings never change is what you find,
The comfort and unexpected friendly chaos feel
like home
The gateway of a vacation becomes a stress-free
walk and roam

And once again we are sitting together
On the rocks and beaches
Sipping drinks and laughing as no time has
passed

I am waiting for you at bus stop

Woke up to my alarm at 5 in the morning
To get ready and catch the college bus
I see you smiling and waiting at the stop
And while we wait for the bus to arrive
Of all the talks we have,
You give me a valuable advice
"Somedays we ask for things to not happen far
too many times",
"That we forget to ask what we want in our life"
The bus soon arrives, and in we board
Forgetting all that was said in the crowd

Few years later, I find myself standing at the
stop
But do not find you there waiting for me
wearing your usual flipflops
I watch the empty seat beside me
But no one to give me a valuable lesson for free
The words ring true as the time passes,
I ask myself what I overlooked to ask in those
days
Now that I miss your companionship
All I had asked was for "I will never lose a
friend like you"

But now I realize,
That what I asked was wrong and untrue
It was never about losing a friendship,
It was asking for "I will make the best of these
moments that I will spend with you"
I hear a honk faraway and find myself break
away from the trance
I board the bus, but through the window I see a
girl lingering from the past
A shadow of me still sitting on those seats
waiting for you at the bus stop

Long distance

We hear about the romantic interludes and
long-distance relationships,
But what about those friends that scatter like
dandelions for their jobs and families?
What about those friends,
Who still decide to do long-distance friendships
To planning calls for every week,
And a group video call every month
We find ourselves in a position to fight against
time,
For a text from our known friend that's gone to
earn every dime

Weeks turns to months
Once in blue moon a text comes
And you ponder how much things have really
changed
Even though we have advanced from letters to
mobiles and the numbers exchanged
The time we wished we could have saved
Is now with no excuses trailed with the feelings
of being depraved
With the increasing distance,
We realize the loss of persistence

But nobody said it was easy to follow up on a
long-distance friendship
Because there are days when the phone still
rings,
From those faraway friends, who merrily talk
like a new life and spring

Cozy weekends

Some of us are outgoing,
While some of us like staying-in
To all treks, strolls on beaches and clubbing,
There exists a cozy bedroom and our favorite
movie waiting
Even with our most stunning ways of dressing,
In each other's company, we still prefer pj's as
comforting

There is nothing like a coffee, a movie and a
friend besides,
Talking, giggling, and crying with the tissues
aside
We may not move from the cozy comfort in
which we are,
Meanwhile time spins its wheel so far
And then we see the sun set down,
It's an end of a beautiful weekend we realize
with a frown
With time to depart, we wonder how we lost
track of the hours fly by
It was the presence of a friend who has said it's
good-bye

Breakup therapy

I receive a call, and hear a sniffing sound from
the other side
"It's over", you say in the smallest of voice
I feel pain for you
In the way you convey and seem so blue
Immediately I start gathering my things together
and catch the next cab

I ring the bell and wait anxiously
You open the door, and I came face to face with
sorrowful eyes
My friend who has always been laughter and
sunshine
Has teary eyes like clouds on rainy days
I instantly pull you over and hug you
I hear no sound,
But I don't have to, since I feel the shaking of
that hugging body
I feel my heart break for you

In we go and talk
or more like have a blubbering session full of
tissues and sobs
I see you calm down

And hear myself say "It's going to be fine. I am
with you"
Even though deep down I know it won't for a
long time
To cheer you up, I plan to order your favorite tub
of ice cream
And make a fort of blankets
As we watch the TV mindlessly,
I hear you snore beside me
I pull the blanket over you and me
And find myself slipping into slumber hoping
for things turn right for you to see

Mundane conversations

To every important conversation we have
There is an equivalent mundane conversation we
drag
Meeting friends or having a phone call,
Not every time we talk is something
monumental for long haul
Somedays all we prefer is to talk about those
mundane details of life
That we practice and follow in our own time
And discuss and banter over things that don't
work right
But in the end still follow the same advice
without going in a fight
It feels great to just describe those routines
That we know about each other since we were
teens
But, hey who said you cannot talk about
mundane conundrum
With a friend who will willingly smile and hear
our tantrums

Seasons of Friendships

I met a friend in summer,
Full of laughter, sunshine, and eyes with
glimmer,
I met a friend when it rained,
A little somber, collected and self-contained
I met a friend in autumn when leaves turn
brown,
Well poised, secretive with a slight frown
I met a friend in winter when it's blinding white
A good listener who preferred to stay quiet
I met a friend in spring when life is out and
about
Who was fun and brought mirth in my life
without a doubt

Do you remember?

Do you remember the first time we met?
Because I marvel if it was a coincidence or fate
Do you remember the first time we went out to
eat?
Because I vividly see you eating burger on my
adjoining seat
Do you remember about our favorite place
where we spent time talking and gossiping?
Because I remember that place was where our
friendship was blossoming
Do you remember the first time you decided to
pick me up for a ride?
Because I still feel air in my hair when I sat
behind
Do you remember the call you made about your
breakup?
Because I still hear the deep sob and hiccups
Do you remember you sharing the news of your
first job?
That glow on your face and hardly containing
glee made me happy and my heart throb
Do you remember about sharing with me about
finding "The one "
The wonder and happiness in your voice as
bright as sun

Now as we wait on the threshold of new years of
this life
Would you remember all of this when we are old
and away from strife?

Impromptu plans

We are sitting in the cafeteria one evening with
our plates full
Suddenly you hear one of them say "Let's go for
a night hike that's chill and cool"
You feel a resounding "no" bubble up in you
But something tells you "Don't be that friend
who flops the plan and screws"
"It's a ride in the evening wake" you think
What could be so different and go wrong in a
blink?
The entire group leaves and hops on the bike
The engine burps up and you find yourself
fascinated about the hike
It's late night by the time we reach beneath the
stretching trails
All packed up and secretly wondering what it
entails
Up we follow the trails and start hiking
With lots of jokes, stories, and continuous
chattering
It's mid of the night when we reach the top
We make a bonfire and sit beside each with a
plop
And then the music and games are played

Years later all I remember is the light from the bonfire dancing on your smiling faces and the night owls serenade

Talks during our walks

It started with a "Let's go for a walk, I want to
tell you something",
To becoming a part of our everyday regimen
Now there are days when we talk all the way
long
And days when we just share comfortable
silences with birds singing their songs
From animatedly talking about an exciting day
To deeply discussing the problems all the way
Some days we find solutions through our talk
Or find an inspiration for our new project during
this walk
Be the trouble about a job, lover, or family
matter
By the end of the walk, we do feel better
What is to say, with each step we take
Might be a friendship builds in its wake

Our sacred space

I found a sacred space, where I could be myself
But what I wanted was to share it with a noble
friend like thyself
Hesitant as I was to let anybody know about it
After some contemplation, this was the place we
decided to meet
And so many core memories were formed here
I am glad I decided to show it as it was now or
never

With the slipping sand in the hourglass,
Left some of its grains back as these memories
of the past
I now happen to have those stories we shared
And laughter, mirth we carried by letting our
souls bared
Nevertheless, in the dreams I visit this place,
And find you are already waiting in our sacred
space

5 Love Language of Friendships

They said, "For your friends, say words of affirmations",
I said "My friends bestowed me with loyalty, kindness, and affection"
They said, "With your friends, spend quality time",
I said "My friends created a safe space for us to bring our troubles and contentment at prime"
They said, "Make sure to share and receive gifts",
I said "My friends continue to give me surprises and random visits"
They asked about "Acts of service towards each other"
I said "I am grateful to them for the calls which were irrelevant to significant discussions with one another"
They asked about, "Sharing physical touch as human"
I said "A hug from my friends has always brought me peace and resolved any confusion"

I found a friend in me

From cradles we are looking for establishing
relationships
Whether it be with our parents, siblings or
making new friendships
Somewhere as time passes, we are lost in sea of
people to find something amiss
But what we disregard is that we always had a
friend in ourselves offering us this bliss
A companionship of the body with our soul
That supports us, faces relentless challenges, and
cherishes the achieved goals

A friend who is there for us at 2 am and let us
relive our pain
Or cheer us for our monetary gain
To spiritually grow,
And that lets amity been bestowed
With each step I take, you follow me like a
shadow
I am glad to have found a friend in me for sure I
know

Starry canvas

From sitting beside each other on the benches,
We have come far along, but there is a distance
that now stretches
For some of us it's different time zones
While others it's different jobs and unknowns
I wait for the time when we meet
When the night is dark and like old days we
greet
Just like that a dusty old cover from years old
painting is pulled over
Light shines on the canvas of our reminiscent
past and glory days like it's been a forever,
The words pour like a running stream
As if time will outrun us and wake us from this
beautiful dream
We talk about good old days
And how life is now-a-days
With beer in one hand and other pointing
towards the stars and constellations
We see the darkness pulling its blanket of stars
with each waking moment of our admiration
In silence, somewhere deep down we know that
even if we would be worlds apart
Under the same blanket of stars, we will find our
way back to each other in our heart

Travel Buddies

I was out and about by myself enjoying my
solitary,
Exploring, reflecting, and being curious
involuntarily
I looked beside me and you were sitting by the
tree,
Lost in your own world, but had an aura that
seemed free
I approached you and asked if you belonged
from here,
You said you were travelling and unravelling the
mysteries of the world here and there
You asked me if I was travelling unaccompanied
I said I was by myself till then, but now it seem I
had a company
We talked about the places we had explored and
new insights we had gained
With each word we exchanged, we realized we
were voyagers untamed
For future travels, we decided to stay connected
And parted our ways with our hearts elated
And that's the fun of travelling as a solo
passenger
You never know what the next stop hides as your
new messenger